The Amaz

Contents

written by Pam Holden

mother and joey

Because Australia is isolated from other countries, very few of its native animals are found anywhere else in the world. The most well-known creature is the fascinating kangaroo, which cannot walk or run, but moves about by hopping slowly or bounding fast. It is the only large animal that moves by hopping. Like many other Australian mammals, the kangaroo is a marsupial, which means that the female has a pouch of skin in front of its stomach to carry its babies. The red kangaroo is the largest of more than 50 species, all belonging to the Macropod group of marsupials. Macropod, meaning "bigfoot", is a good description because of its outsized hind feet.

The first explorers visiting the huge Australian continent were astonished to discover many thousands of these unusual animals living there. They found the kangaroo difficult to describe to others on their return, explaining, "It's the size of a man, and often stands tall on its two enormous hind legs. It has a head like a deer, short front legs and a powerful thick tail. With its baby looking out of a pouch on its stomach, it bounds across the plains with an enormous mob moving at great speed."

The most unusual feature of a kangaroo is its strong muscular tail, which it uses in different ways. This large tail acts as a third leg when hopping about. The kangaroo raises its tail for steering and balance when bounding fast on its large back legs. Its short front legs are used like crutches with the tail to balance while hopping slowly. When it stops moving it rests on its tail like a prop, then uses it to push off and start jumping. Injury to a kangaroo's tail is extremely serious, as the animal can't hop with its tail lifted off the ground. Moving about to search for food becomes impossible.

Although a fully-grown red kangaroo can be taller than an adult human, it starts its life as a tiny baby called a joey. It is born after only twelve days inside its mother, when it is smaller than a caterpillar! At birth the tiny pink joey is blind and helpless. It takes about fifteen minutes to crawl unassisted through its mother's soft fur to reach the shelter of her pouch. There it immediately attaches itself to one of her four milk nipples, drinking and developing for twelve weeks. After that time it begins to leave the warmth and safety of the pouch briefly to explore its environment. If it becomes frightened or tired, it hurriedly returns to safety by diving into the pouch head first!

The joey leaves the pouch permanently after eight months, but remains close to its mother, drinking her nourishing milk by putting its head into her pouch to find a teat.

Adults keep a lookout when grazing together, communicating with their joeys and others by stamping their hind feet on the ground to warn of possible danger.

An estimated number of 26 million kangaroos, far outnumbering Australia's human population, live in hot dry areas, where they move over vast distances searching for food sources. Their diet is mainly grass, bark, shoots and leaves, from which they get most of the small amount of water they need. They can live for months without drinking, and when thirsty can reach water by digging wells in the ground.

An amazing spectacle is the sight of kangaroos bounding across desert plains in mobs of hundreds, often reaching a full speed as fast as a racing bike.

Because kangaroos are mostly nocturnal animals, they are often seen resting lazily under shady trees during daytime. Their activity at night causes constant danger for motorists, unable to avoid them as they bound across roads at high speed. Collisions are usually fatal for the kangaroos, while also causing injury to motorists and damage to vehicles. These accidents are a problem that seems impossible to solve. Other dangers for kangaroos are hunters who kill them for their meat and skins, as well as Australia's native wild dogs, called dingoes, which sometimes attack joeys. Eagles can be a threatening enemy to young or injured animals also.

14

lazing roo

The unusual shape of their hind legs and their bulky tails make it difficult for these animals to walk or move backwards easily. Another strange fact about kangaroos is that they can't move their two back legs independently of each other except when swimming. They can swim strongly across rivers, in dams and the ocean, kicking each leg separately.

Two males sometimes fight, leaning back on their strong tails to balance as they stand on their hind legs boxing each other. They attack by jabbing with their front legs, biting, scratching with their sharp claws, and kick-boxing with their hind legs.

Their name is often shortened to "roos", with males known as boomers, bucks or jacks, and females called flyers, does or jills. All young marsupials are known as joeys, including koalas, wallabies, and opossums.

The suggestion that a kangaroo could live up a tree seems unbelievable, but there is a species called a tree kangaroo that lives high in tall treetops of tropical forests. It is an excellent climber and walks along branches to feed on fruit, nuts, moss, leaves and flowers. It can move with enormous jumps down to the ground without hurting itself, as well as leaping long distances from tree to tree.

tree kangaroo

The red kangaroo also has an amazing jump – it can leap as high as a bus! At full speed its bounds can measure more than the width of a road!

Anyone who has seen or studied the kangaroo must agree that it is an incredible creature!